Insincerely
yours,

Insincerely yours,

CARTOONS BY

DANA FRADON

CHARLES SCRIBNER'S SONS • NEW YORK

Library of Congress Cataloging in Publication Data

Fradon, Dana.
   Insincerely yours
   Cartoons from the New Yorker Magazine.
   1. American wit and humor, Pictorial. I. Title.
NC1429.F6648A4 1978   741.5′973   78-5030
ISBN 0-684-15578-8

1 3 5 7 9 11 13 15 17 19 M/C 20 18 16 14 12 10 8 6 4 2

PRINTED IN THE UNITED STATES OF AMERICA

To JAMES GERAGHTY

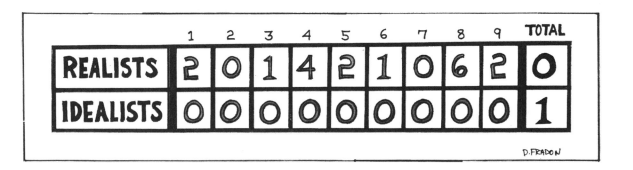

Preface

The drawings in this book are primarily meant to make you laugh. I hope they also make some small comment on a few of the not-so-funny problems we seem to manufacture for ourselves on this otherwise beautiful, bountiful, and essentially benign planet.

More persistent than radioactive waste, our self-inflicted problems seem to have a half-life of forever. We like to think they get better as time goes by, but this is only an illusion. In most cases we simply learn to live with them. At times we sincerely believe we've eliminated some of the little rascals, but they quickly mutate and come back to haunt us in some other form.

What motivates one cartoonist to do amusing drawings about cats, dogs, husbands, and wives, and another to delve into bribes, kickbacks, and political hacks? James Geraghty, the former *New Yorker* cartoon editor, after looking at one of my submissions that was extremely hard on the Establishment but revealed precious little warmth for the "little guy," said to me, "Let's face it, Dana, you're not motivated by any love for the oppressed, you're motivated by hatred of the oppressor!"

Taken with a grain of salt, or salt substitute, it was a correct analysis.

As the saying goes, "In a democracy, you gets the kind of government (and, I might add, society) you deserve." In the last analysis, the people must accept responsibility for the problems in their society. Politicians keep repeating the same promises to cure the same ills. Very often, when pursuing office a second or third time, they can actually be found running against their own previous lack of accomplishment. The citizenry usually accepts it. For this reason it is difficult to be filled with love for the people.

While I limit my anger to those in the saddle, I hold both leaders and followers up to a single set of standards—mine! Ironically enough, these standards come from the mouthings of the very people I pick on. The society I seek is the society given lip service to by one and all. Governed by the Boy Scout Oath, the West Point Oath, and the Golden Rule, it is populated by nobody but warm-hearted TV Waltons and protected from harm by honest Starskys and Hutches.

A final note: I do not consider this book to be a fantasy comment on something called the "real world." No way! I contend that *my* world, as presented in the next 150 pages, is the real "real world"; the *other* one is fantasy. In these drawings I try to depict people as they really are. I expose them, dissect them, deflate them, vent my spleen on them. And what is their response?

They laugh.

Dana Fradon

NEWTOWN, CONNECTICUT

THE WASHINGTON SCENE

The Citizens

*"Do you ever have days when you can't seem
to rise above petty politics?"*

"Miss Kent, I want that researched, analyzed, verified, encoded, translated, extrapolated, condensed, and typed in triplicate."

"No, no, Miss Clark! I asked you to bring in the Mantle of
Greatness, not the Cloak of Secrecy."

"*My mail seems to be running about three to one against everything!*"

"*Take this, Henderson, and hide it from the public.*"

"*I don't have friends. I just have cronies.*"

"If I'd lived back then, I would have signed it, too."

"*Meaningless statistics were up one-point-five percent
this month over last month.*"

"Damn it, Robinson! You call this a plan of action worthy of a great people?"

"Father, I cannot tell a lie."

"Frank, this is Gil Parker, one of the Administration's leading apologists."

THE WASHINGTON SCENE
The Military

*"I ask you! If <u>I</u> had been a
conscientious objector, where would I be today?"*

"Will you please quit saying, 'War is too important to leave to us generals'!"

*"Which of all the wars you've been in would you
say you liked the best?"*

THE WASHINGTON SCENE

The Spooks

"We're in luck. He's in."

"It seems the CIA has not been inactive in this area."

THE LEGAL SCENE

"*I feel I give them their thirty-two thousand five hundred dollars' worth of justice every year.*"

"*Remember, son, we are a government of
loopholes, and not of men!*"

"Do you solemnly swear to tell the truth, the whole truth, and nothing but the truth in exchange for immunity?"

"*I'm happy to say that my final judgment of a case is almost
always consistent with my prejudgment of the case.*"

"Lock him up and throw away the key!"

THE TELEVISION SCENE

"Harrison, do you see what I see in the dancing flames?"

"Closing averages on the human scene were mixed today. Brotherly love was down two points, while enlightened self-interest gained a half. Vanity showed no movement, and guarded optimism slipped a point in sluggish trading. Overall, the status quo remained unchanged."

"*This is the seven-o'clock news with Jim Holton, forty-five thousand dollars a year, in Hong Kong; Pearl Wanda, thirty-seven thousand five hundred dollars, in Alaska; Fred Hutchins, seventy-five thousand dollars, in San Francisco . . .*"

"*I deem thee newsworthy.*"

THE BIG CITY SCENE

"To the Housing Authority, Port Authority, Tunnel Authority, Transit Authority, Bridge Authority—to authority!"

THE BIG BUSINESS SCENE

"Miss Clark, get me the paper shuffler who shuffled these papers!"

" 'Insincerely yours, Fred Troutman.' "

"I have to take one three times a day to curb
my insatiable appetite for power."

"*Damn it, Felton! Stop passing me money under
the table while I'm eating!*"

"*Did you hear about poor Walston? He was consumed by ambition.*"

"Looks like there's some truth to the rumor we're being taken over by Boise Cascade."

"To close on an upbeat note, I'm happy to report we received twenty-two percent more in kickbacks than we paid out in bribes."

*"Damn it, fellows! Someone has got to remember
where we hid the hidden assets."*

"Now, don't accept any bribes or kickbacks, don't engage in false or misleading advertising, don't practice unethical accounting methods . . ."

"OK. Whose turn is it to set the moral tone?"

THE LABOR SCENE

*"Before I do anything, say anything, or try anything, I say to
myself, 'Is it in the best interests of baseball?'"*

"*Those must have been great days when our daddies could press down upon the brow of labor a crown of thorns and crucify mankind upon a cross of gold.*"

"I love every square foot of this great country of ours, except for the liberal Northeast."

THE MEDICAL SCENE

*"Take one of these every four hours. If pain
persists, see another doctor."*

"Damn! I suppose this means another malpractice suit!"

"*Hadn't you best drop in?*"

"*You should take it easy for a while, Mr. Harner. You've been infected by the virus of hate.*"

"*Let me give you a little free advice.*"

THE CRIME IN THE STREETS SCENE

"*I can't say I like the looks of that bunch*"

"If we pull this off, we've made burglary history!"

"*Now listen, Murphy! You've paid your debt to society, so get out of here!*"

INTERMISSION

"*Everybody laughed except that lousy melancholy Dane.*"

"He loves me for myself, he loves me for my body . . ."

"*Why, this broth we made is magnificent!*"

"*Good evening, Mr. Benson. This is a recording calling.*"

"*He's got my eyes and your trunk.*"

"They're guaranteed for as long as the sun shall rise and the rivers flow."

"*Quick! Is that the Earl of Sussex, the Duke of Essex, the Earl of Essex, or the Duke of Sussex?*"

"It's finally happened, Mr. Cramer. 'They' are here to see you."

"Remember, there is no such thing as a small job. There are only small men."

"Hi! I'm Marty Clark."

Why does a fireman wear red suspenders?

A. ☐ *The red goes well with the blue uniform.*
B. ☐ *They can be used to repair a leaky hose.*
C. ☐ *To hold up his pants.*

"I used to be the village idiot until that crumb showed up."

THE MIDDLE-AMERICA SCENE

"I often have an urge these days to stand up and
be counted, but I don't know what for."

"Will they close the banks?"

*"I'll tell you what I see in the dancing flames. I see logs that cost
ninety-five dollars a cord, that's what I see."*

"*You are no different from anyone else.*"

"And here's an extra 'substantial penalty' for the early withdrawal of your time deposit!"

"Oh, stop worrying about humanity's problems! Let humanity worry about its own problems!"

"*Darling, our first loan!*"

*"Would you mind turning down your damn alpha waves
a little? I'm <u>trying</u> to read!"*

"Now, will this be cash or credit?"

"*To your mental health!*"

"*There should be a Hall of Fame for nobodies.*"

"It's the one thing that sustains him."

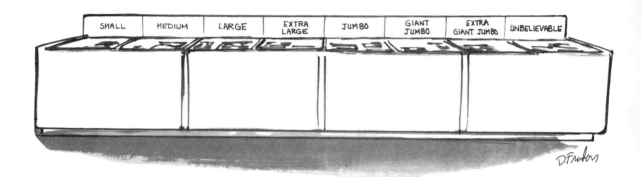

*"Shall we go to Burger Joint, Burger King, Hamburger Hut, McDonald's,
or do you want to stay home and have a hamburger?"*

"For what it's worth, next week all your stars and planets will be in good aspect for you to launch an invasion of England."

"*Do you have something a little more garish? We're nouveaux riches.*"

"Oh, that wasn't me talking. It was the alcohol talking."

THE RICH GET RICHER AND
THE POOR GET POORER SCENE

"If God hadn't wanted there to be poor people, He would
have made us rich people more generous."

"*For God's sake! Pick up your <u>own</u> damn money!*"

"It's not what you know, it's who you know.
And who do I know? You!"

"And I feel I must call to your attention that my prayers of February 6th, 8th, and 19th, as well as those of March 3rd and 4th, have not as yet been answered."

"I admit my cup is full, but it __never__ runneth over."

"*Remember, my boy, never trust anyone.*"
"*Not even Walter Cronkite?*"

"*In that case, how about a weekend at your firm's hunting lodge?*"

"I guess we should count our blessings."

*"Of course, when you seasonally adjust me, I suppose
I'm better off than I think I am."*

"*I was so relieved to find out he was only a phony liberal.*"

"Somehow it seems to miss the true spirit of Christmas."

THE FEMINIST SCENE

"Founding Fathers! How come no Founding Mothers?"

"*Man! I'll bet Gloria Steinem would really flip if she knew we'd voted her the girl we'd most like to be marooned with on a desert island.*"

THE ENVIRONMENTAL SCENE

"Damn right-wingers!"

"*And grant that I may take into my system only acceptable levels of mercury, cadmium, lead, and sulfur dioxide.*"

"To meet the energy shortage as it applies to air conditioning, the panes of glass are so designed that they can be moved up or down—at the occupant's will—thus allowing fresh, cool air to enter the building when desired."

"My God! There are traces of tuna fish in this shipment of mercury!"

"Notice how bright and white Brand X gets your clothing because of the harmful chemicals and enzymes it contains. Pure-O, on the other hand, containing no harmful ingredients, leaves your clothes lackluster gray but protects your environment."

THE ELECTION CAMPAIGN SCENE

"*The Democrats seem to have this district pretty well sewed up.*"

"*They say to get elected to public office in America one must*
be rich. Well, my friends, I'm rich. I'm very rich."

"How many times have you asked yourself, 'What can I, as a single person, possibly do to help shape the destiny of mankind?' Well, I'll tell you what you can do. You can vote for me."

"I'm climbing steadily in the polls. A recent survey had me first
in war, second in peace, and first in the hearts of my countrymen."

*"If the election were held today, who would
you reluctantly vote for?"*

THE INCOME TAX SCENE

"You'll be happy to know that nobody in the government is out to get you, nobody's reported you for the finder's fee, nor have we received any anonymous tips. You're here only because we think you've been cheating on your return."

"What do you mean, 'clarify miscellaneous'? What do you think that word is for?"

"I'd hate to tell you how much I'm going to have
to render unto Caesar this year."

THE CHURCH SCENE

"Do you have any idea <u>when</u> the meek shall inherit the earth?"

"Of course, if national security is involved,
disregard everything I've said."

"*Mark my words. Let priests <u>marry</u>, and the next thing they'll want is <u>divorce</u>.*"

"And let us remember—that which we render unto God is deductible from that which we render unto Caesar."

THE SOUTH AMERICAN SCENE

*"When a Communist can win a free election, I say
there's something wrong with free elections!"*

THE SUPER-PATRIOT SCENE

"Harry, any discount to a super-patriot?"

"What do you mean, 'My country, right or wrong'? Just when has our country ever been wrong?"

THE PORN SCENE

"Arise, Sir Myron Besner, King of Porn."

THE INTELLECTUAL COMMUNITY SCENE

*"I can't put it into layman's language for you. I don't
know any layman's language."*

"Shakespeare, Marlowe, Bacon, Pope, Swift, Pepys, Dryden, Chaucer, Milton, Aristophanes, Euripides, Cervantes, Donne, Goethe, Blake, Schiller, Keats, Byron, Johnson, Moore, Emerson—Uh, I've forgotten the point I was going to make."

He's one of the top ten laymen in the country."

*"Damn you, Winkle, did you have to go and ask it
which came first—the chicken or the egg?"*

THE MADISON AVENUE SCENE

"There goes what I would call an adman's adman."

"And now, before we proceed to the next canvas, we pause in our commentary to bring you this message. Featured in our fourth-floor cafeteria today is our special chef's salad—one dollar and forty cents, beverage and dessert included."

"Have they no shame?"

THE INVESTMENT SCENE

*"Did it ever occur to you that I might not be
jumping for economic reasons?"*

"God bless everything on the New York Stock Exchange, and on the American Stock Exchange, and all those little over-the-counter stocks."

157

"*Oh-oh! I don't like the looks of this!*"

THE LAST SCENE

"George, this is the late Fred Warner. Fred, this is the late George Edwards."